TV Themes

Arranged by Dan Coates

CONTENTS

Cover Image © iStockphoto.com/nodmitry

Copyright © MMIX by Alfred Music Publishing Co., Inc.
All Rights Reserved   Printed in USA
ISBN-10: 0-7390-6170-4
ISBN-13: 978-0-7390-6170-1

Alfred

BATMAN THEME

Batman

Words and Music by Neal Hefti
Arranged by Dan Coates

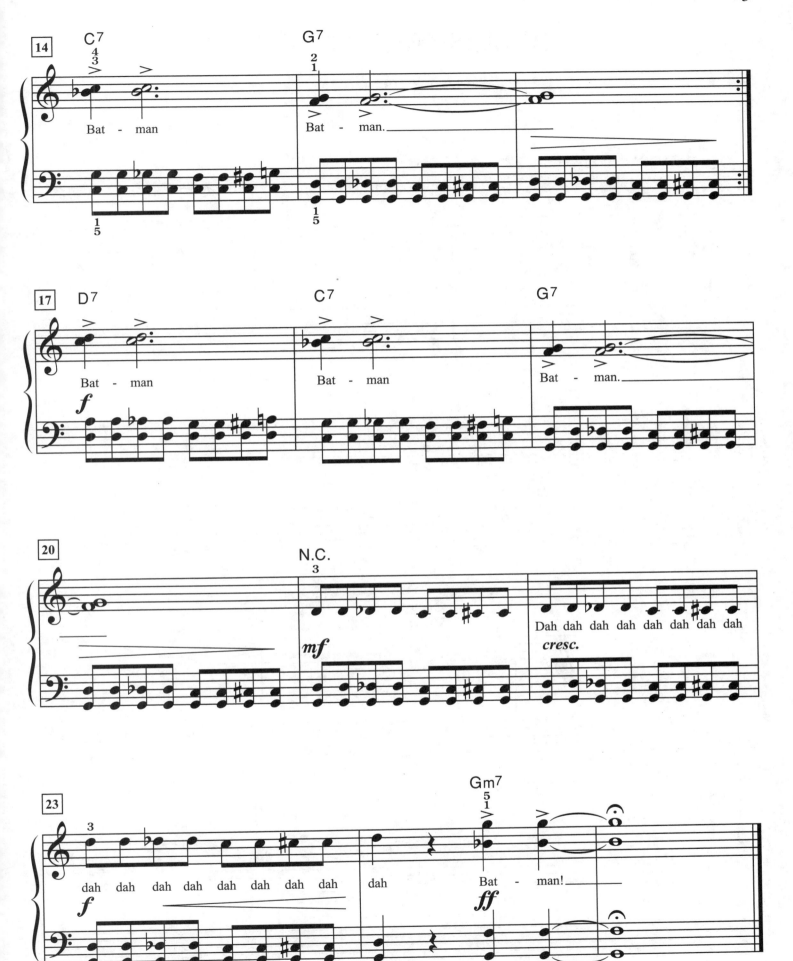

HILL STREET BLUES

Hill Street Blues

Music by Mike Post
Arranged by Dan Coates

THE BALLAD OF GILLIGAN'S ISLE

Gilligan's Island

Words and Music by
Sherwood Schwartz and George Wyle
Arranged by Dan Coates

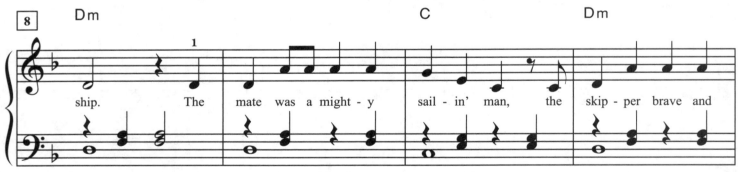

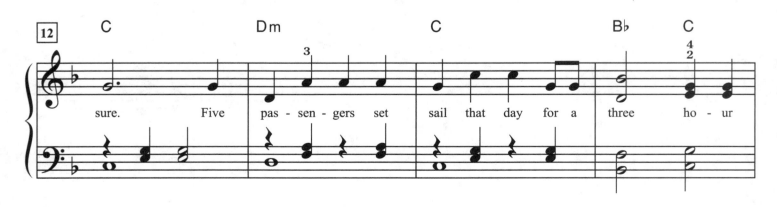

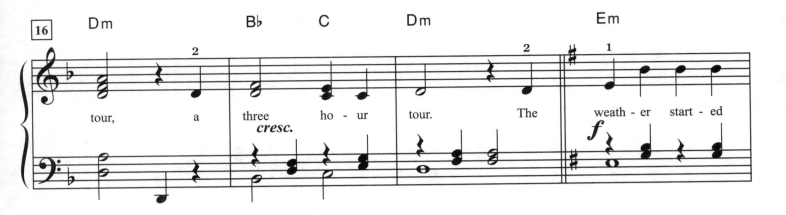

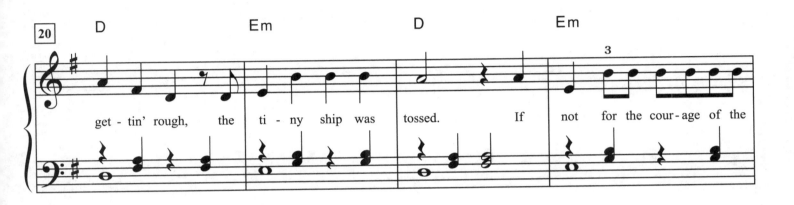

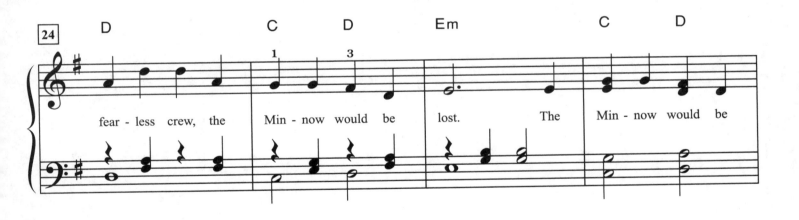

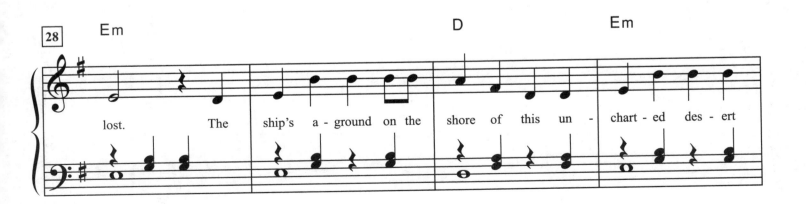

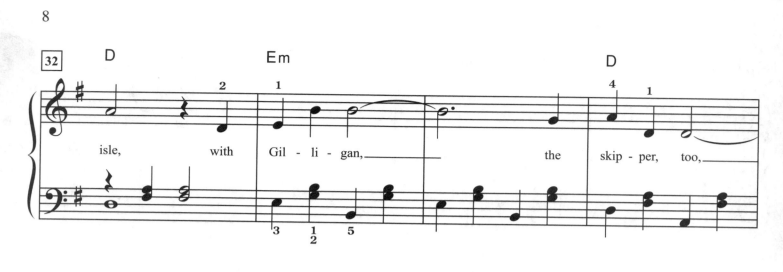

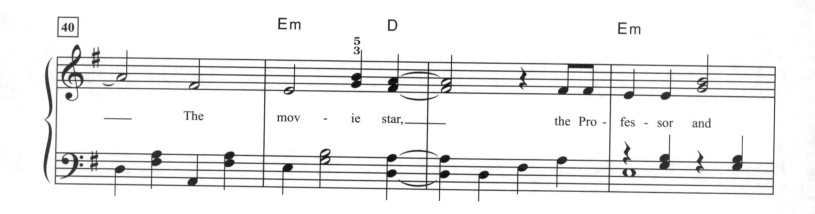

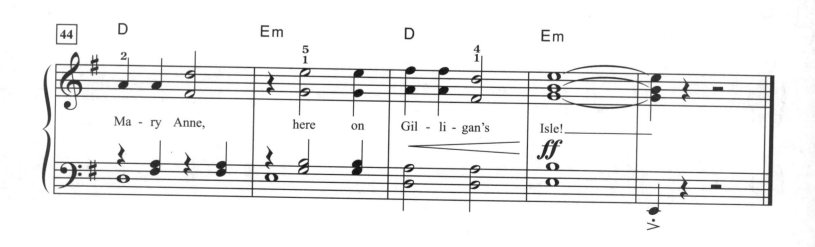

I'LL BE THERE FOR YOU

Friends

Words by David Crane, Marta Kauffman,
Allee Willis, Phil Solem and Danny Wilde
Music by Michael Skloff
Arranged by Dan Coates

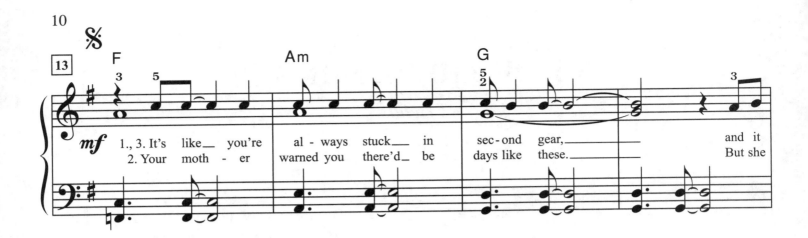

1., 3. It's like__ you're al - ways stuck__ in sec - ond gear,_____ and it
2. Your moth - er warned you there'd__ be days like these._____ But she

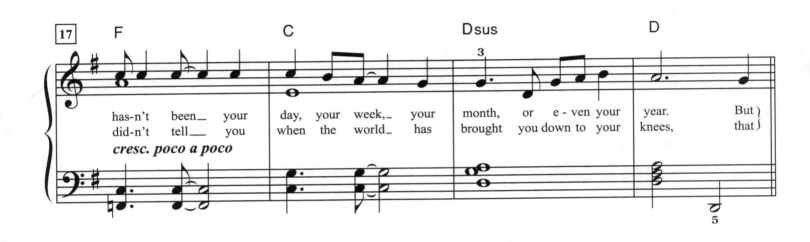

has-n't been__ your day, your week,__ your month, or e - ven your year. But
did-n't tell__ you when the world__ has brought you down to your knees, that

cresc. poco a poco

Chorus:

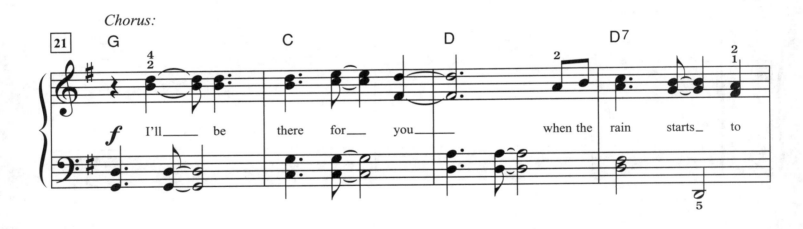

I'll____ be there for__ you____ when the rain starts__ to

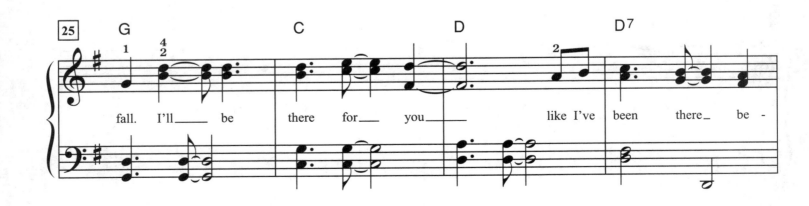

fall. I'll____ be there for__ you____ like I've been there be -

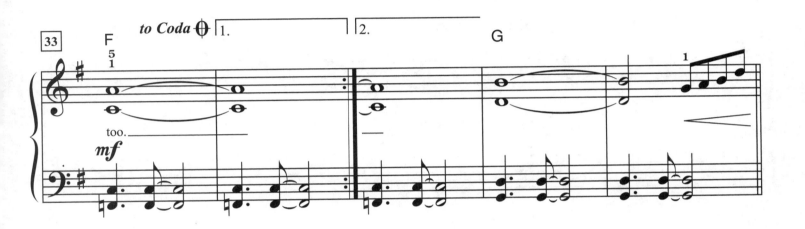

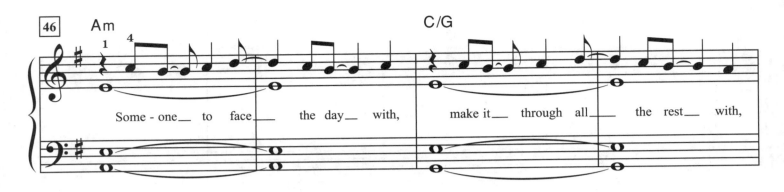

Some-one__ to face__ the day__ with, make it__ through all__ the rest__ with,

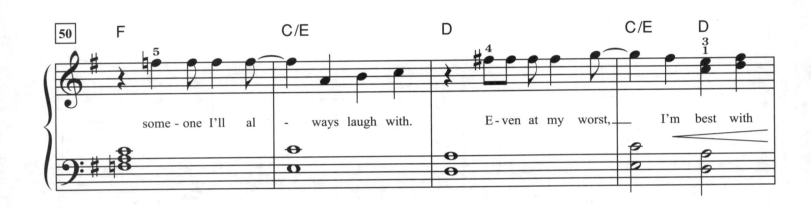

some-one I'll al - ways laugh with. E-ven at my worst,__ I'm best with

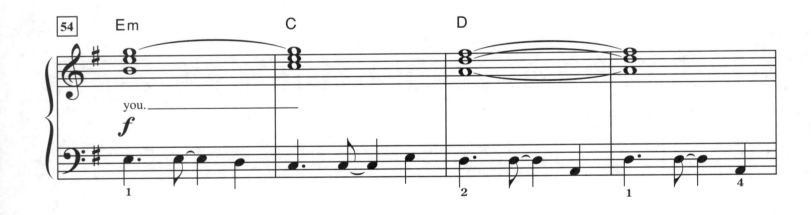

you.__

D.S. al Coda

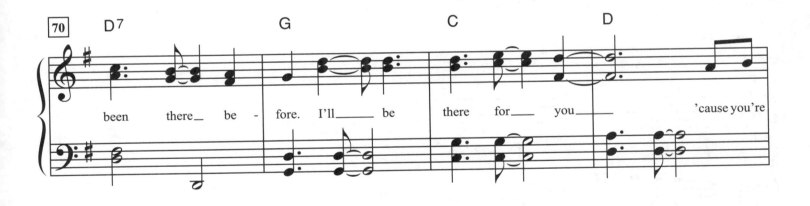

INSPECTOR GADGET (MAIN TITLE)

Inspector Gadget

Words and Music by
Haim Saban and Shuki Levy
Arranged by Dan Coates

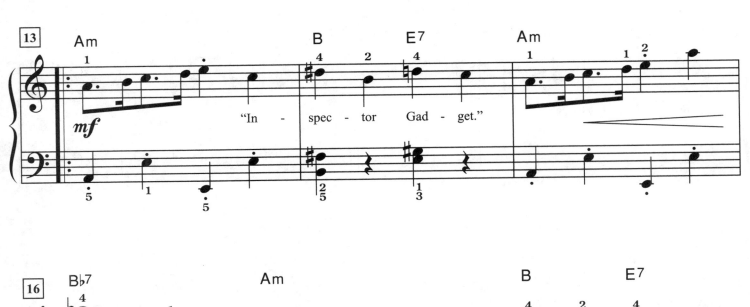

"In - spec - tor Gad - get."

"In - spec - tor Gad - get."

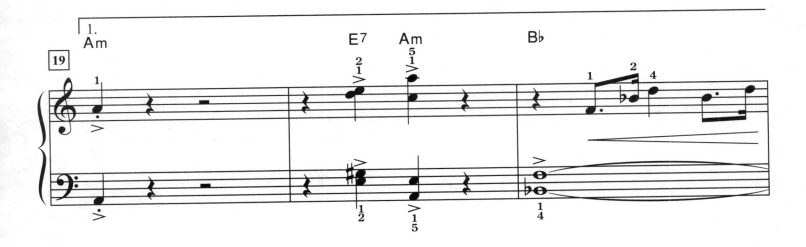

"Go, Gad - get, go."

"Go, Gad - get, go."

"In -

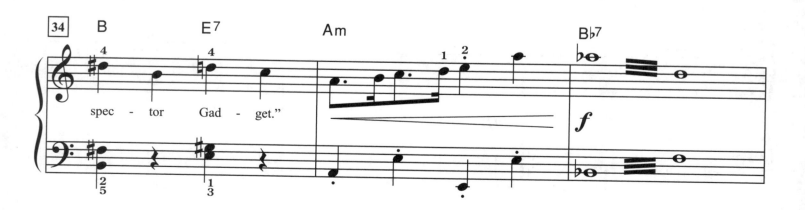

spec - tor Gad - get."

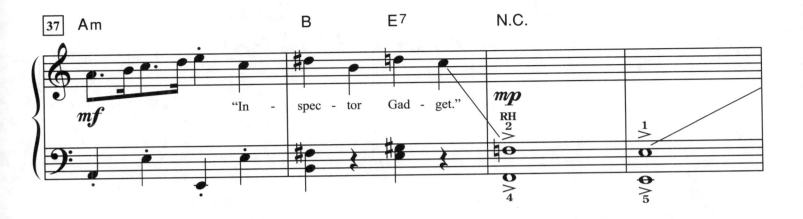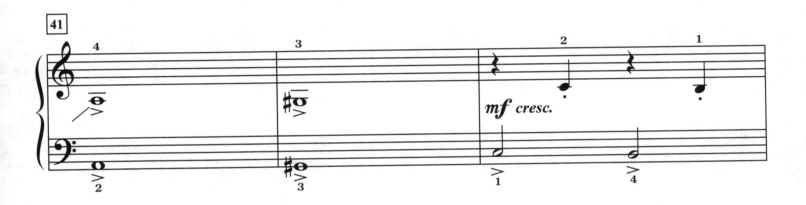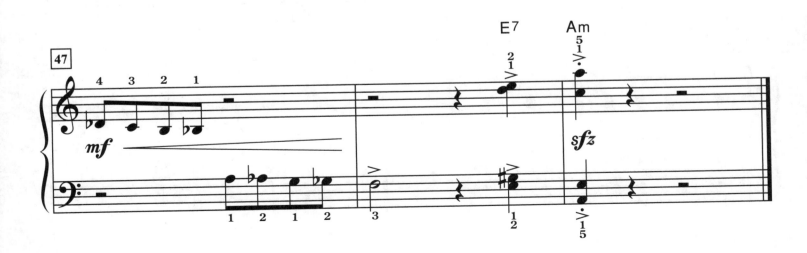

SONG FROM M*A*S*H
(SUICIDE IS PAINLESS)

*M*A*S*H*

Words and Music by
Mike Altman and Johnny Mandel
Arranged by Dan Coates

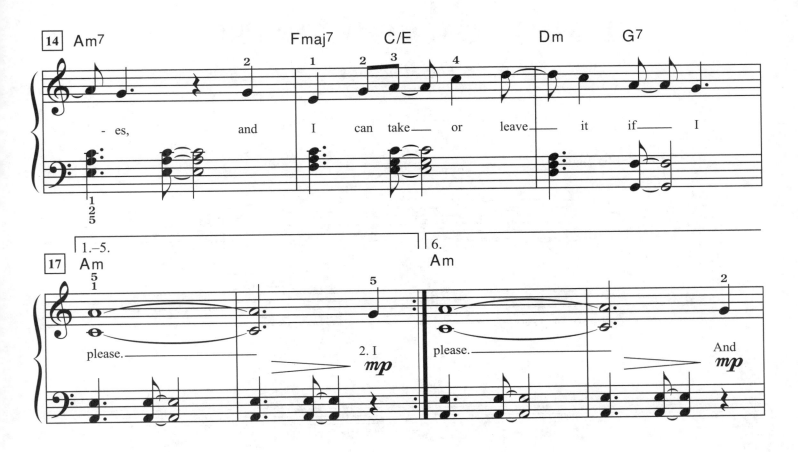

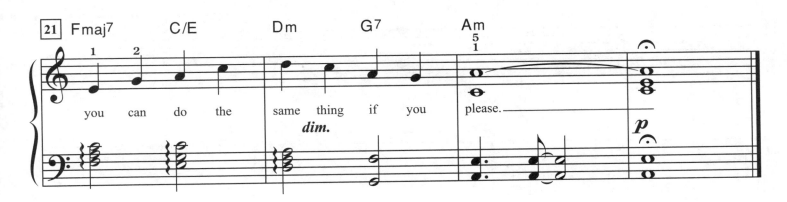

Verse 2:
I try to find a way to make
All our little joys relate
Without that ever-present hate
But now I know that it's too late.
And *(To Chorus:)*

Verse 3:
The game of life is hard to play,
I'm going to lose it anyway,
The losing card I'll someday lay,
So that is all I have to say,
That *(To Chorus:)*

Verse 4:
The only way you win is cheat,
And lay it down before I'm beat,
And to another give a seat,
For that's the only painless feat.
'Cause *(To Chorus:)*

Verse 5:
The sword of time will pierce our skins,
It doesn't hurt when it begins,
But as it works its way on in
The pain grows stronger, watch it grin.
For *(To Chorus:)*

Verse 6:
A brave man once requested me
To answer questions that are key,
Is it to be or not to be?
And I replied, "Oh, why ask me?"
'Cause *(To Chorus:)*

THEME FROM "THE SIMPSONS"

The Simpsons

By Danny Elfman
Arranged by Dan Coates

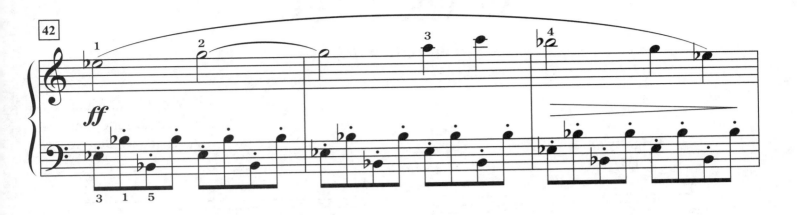

MOVIN' ON UP

The Jeffersons

Words and Music by
Jeff Barry and Janet Dubois
Arranged by Dan Coates

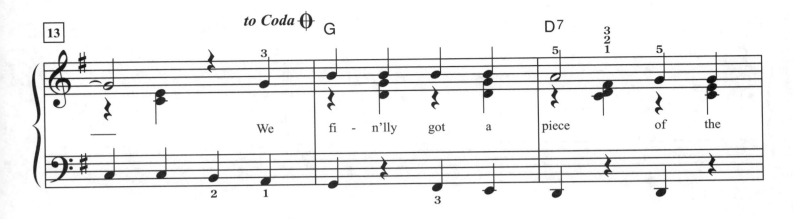

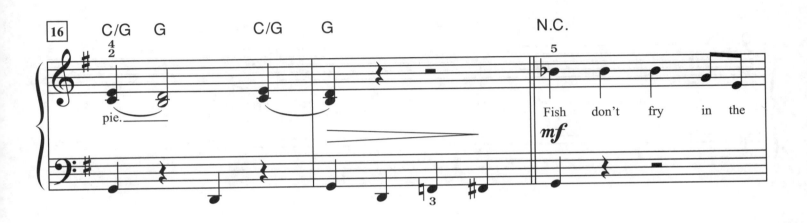

hill. Now we're up___ in the big leagues

get-tin' our turn at bat. As long as we live, it's
cresc.

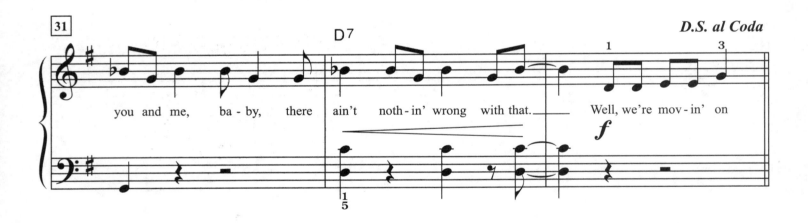

D.S. al Coda

you and me, ba-by, there ain't noth-in' wrong with that.___ Well, we're mov-in' on
f

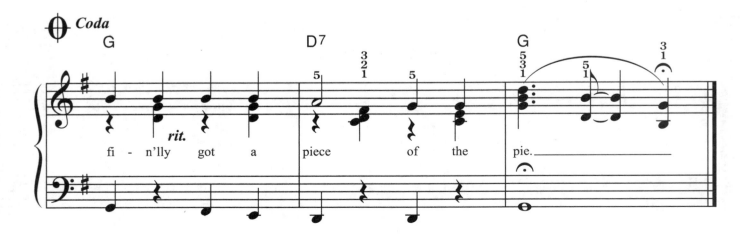

Coda
G

D7

G

rit.

fi - n'lly got a piece of the pie.___

THOSE WERE THE DAYS

All in the Family

Music by Charles Strouse
Words by Lee Adams
Arranged by Dan Coates

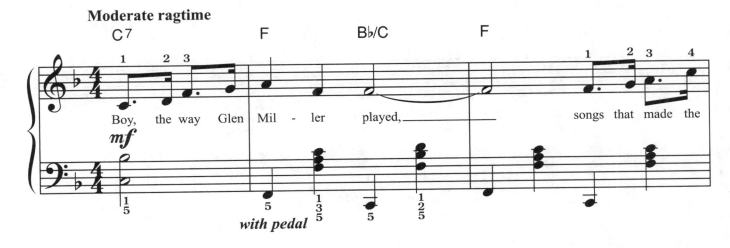

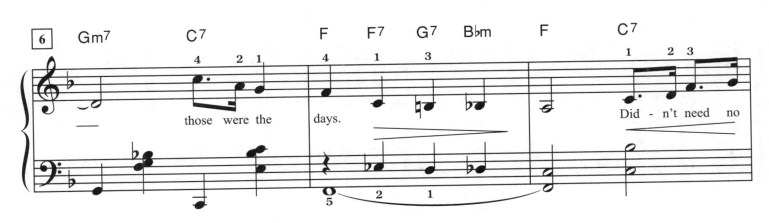

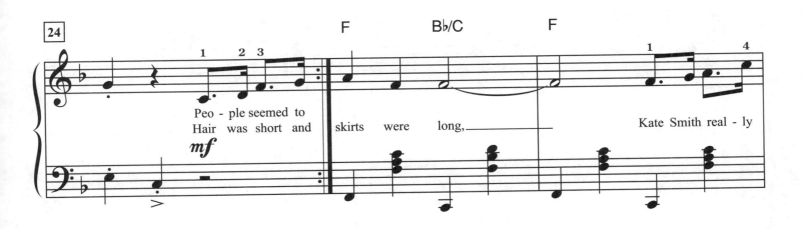

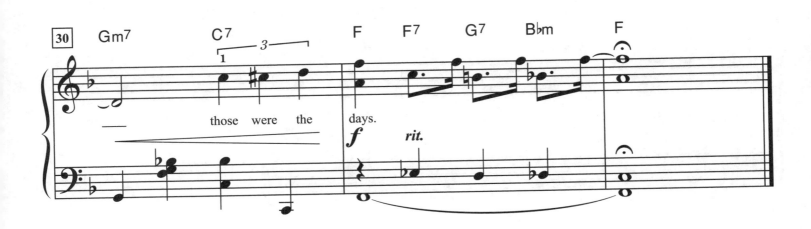

WKRP IN CINCINNATI

WKRP in Cincinnati

Music by Tom Wells
Lyrics by Hugh Wilson
Arranged by Dan Coates

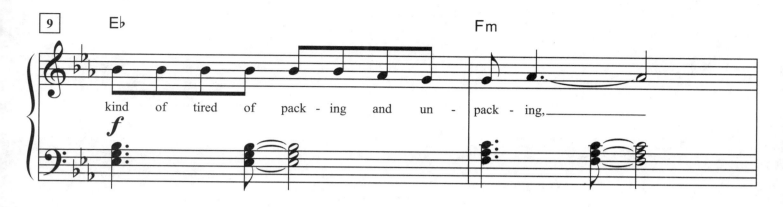

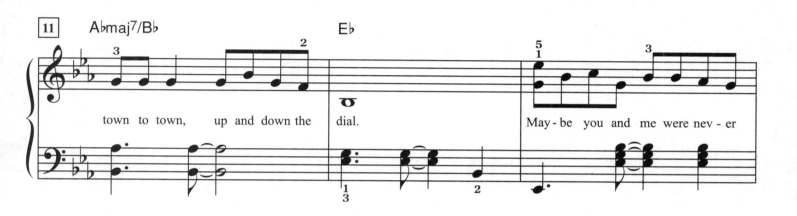

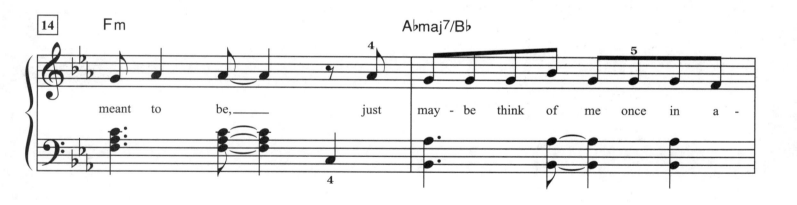

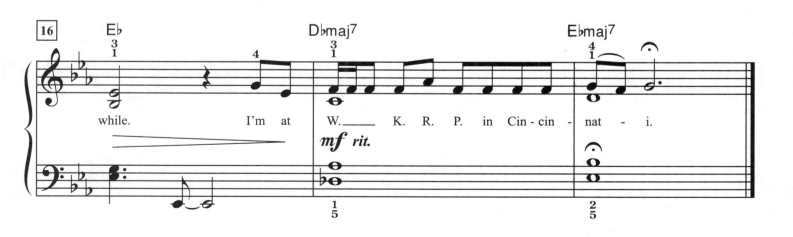